Music Literacy For Everyone

Maeve Smith

Sentience Publications

To Jack

Am I forgetting you?   *Oh No*

Acknowledgement

It means a lot to me to bring this book to market, and I would like to express my heartfelt gratitude to everyone who has either been involved in its production, or whose support and encouragement has contributed to bringing it to fruition. I have thoroughly enjoyed the process of putting it together, and I am excited to share my passion for teaching music to a much wider audience.

Maeve Smith, Ashbourne, 2016

Foreword

Some of my earliest memories take me back to the age of three, when I would sit at our old family piano in Athy, experimenting with what would have been a new and exciting instrument for me. I was amazed that I could play more than one note at a time and totally transform the sound. For that three-year old child, the piano was something enchanting, something in which I could lose myself for hours and keep discovering things anew, simply by pressing different note combinations. I firmly believe that while one can on one's own discover a real love for music, it takes a special type of person to recognise that interest, develop the associated ability and hone the necessary skills. For me, Maeve Smith was that person.

When I first met Maeve back in the early '80s, she was teaching at St. Joseph's School for the Visually Impaired in Dublin (now ChildVision). She cultivated my passion for music, not only by allowing my ear to develop, but also by working with me through Graded examinations with the Royal Irish Academy of Music; and probably most significantly, by introducing me to Music Literacy, through Braille. When I took on a Music Degree at University College Cork in the mid-'90s, I quickly discovered that Braille Music would be the key to its completion. More than that, however, it enabled me to flourish in a mainstream 3rd level Music setting.

My connection with Maeve has lasted beyond that of a pupil and teacher relationship. She has long been a wonderful friend and a guiding presence in my life; not only because of her unique ability to recognise and develop musical talent, but also because of her wisdom and outlook on so many aspects of life.

I was delighted to have played a small part in the development of this book, but I'm honoured to have been asked to write this Foreword. This book will allow those who want to revive long forgotten musical interests to do so, just as it will be a friend to those who have never previously explored music but who think they might like to give it a try. I highly recommend that the reader do exactly what that three-year-old child did: start exploring your own music, see where it takes you, and let Maeve's passion and knowledge accompany you on your journey.

Stuart Lawler
Manager of the Rehabilitation Training Centre with the National Council for the Blind of Ireland

Table of Contents

Introduction

The purpose of this book is to reach out to those people who would gain from a good basic knowledge of music notation. They may not express such desire or they may assume, "I wouldn't manage this," but if the desire for basic music literacy is there as well as the commitment, "Yes, you would."

Those whom I have in mind are young or older adults. They may or may not have learned to play piano or another instrument when younger. Among these and of especial relevance are those who are adept at technology, but limited in their knowledge of music. This combination [music and technology] would go at least some way towards filling a void in to-day's world of music. I do not of course rule out younger people, but if very young they will probably need the aid of a tutor or guide. Some of the happier outcomes for all will be more understanding, confidence and interest as a member of a choir or instrumental group, or in attending concerts.

The book includes *harmony* in that the principal chords used to harmonise are outlined. This is as a natural progression from scales. The pieces are relatively easy, chords being identifiable. The more adventurous may use their own arrangement of these, elaborating on their style.

The programme as set out does not follow a particular exam course, but would—I believe—complement such syllabi as Junior Certificate leading on to Leaving Certificate as well as Royal Irish Academy of Music Theory and Harmony, and other such examinations.

Music is an important element in many people's lives, even if they have not studied the subject formally. To these I would say, a good basic knowledge of music notation will enhance your interest and enjoyment in making and listening to music.

There is a rhythm in life, it is apt that we recognise and fit ourselves to this, and mould and to some extent form this rhythm. Hence, we may more easily embrace new challenges and row along with life.

Chapter 1
Notes and Note Values

Notes

Our notes are C D E F G A B

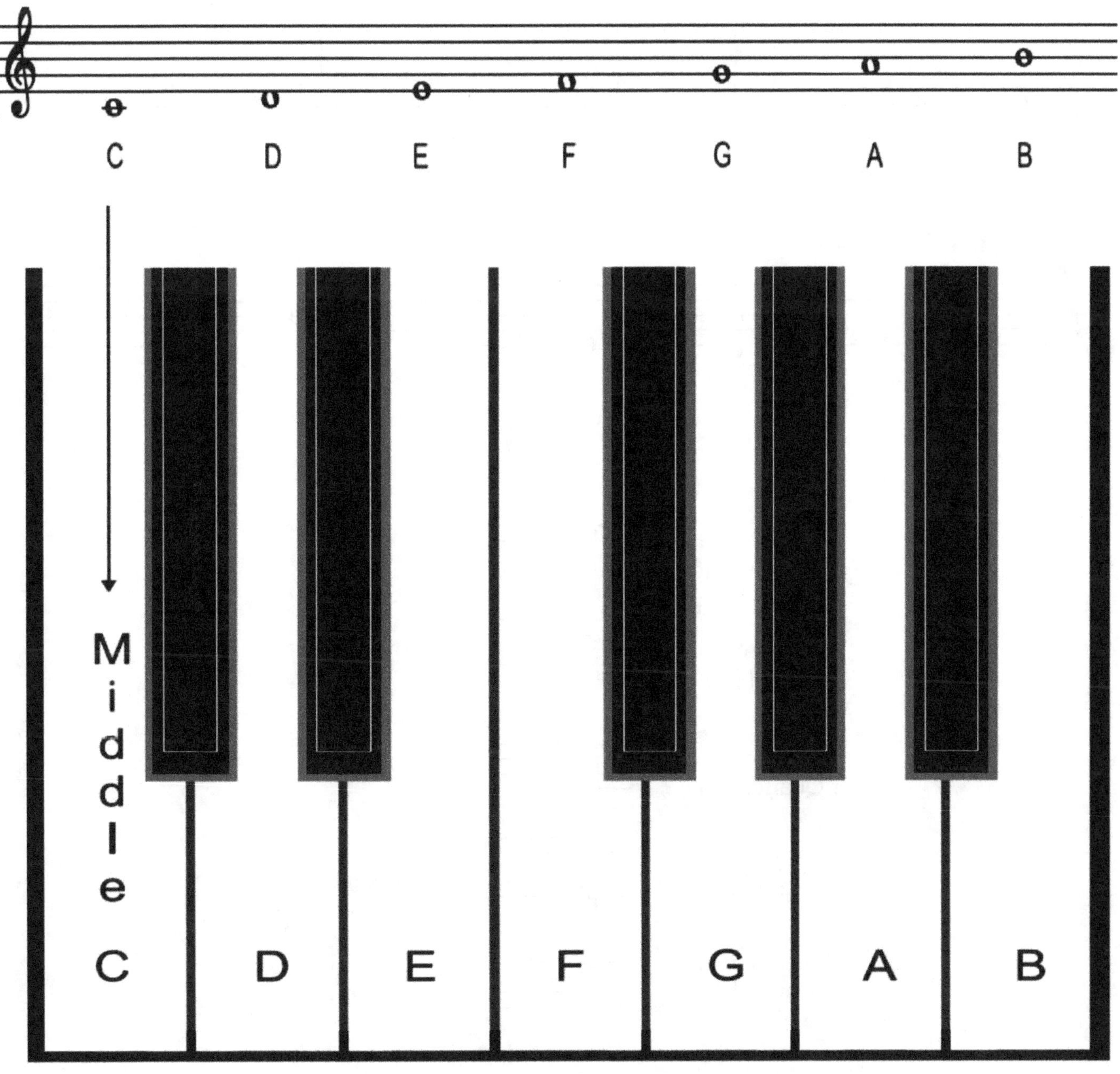

For practice on C D E, name these notes, located in the middle of the keyboard

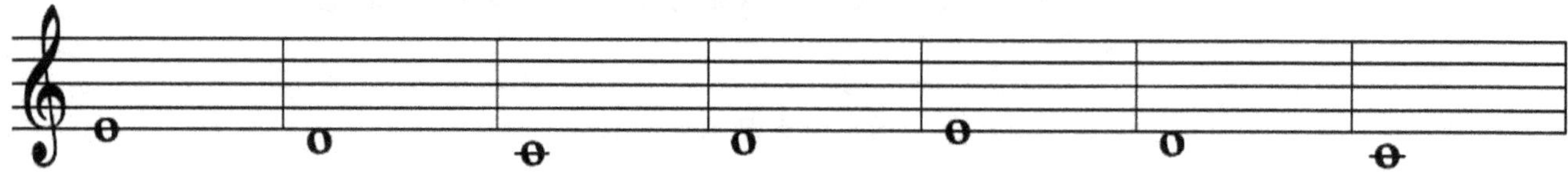

Now F G A B

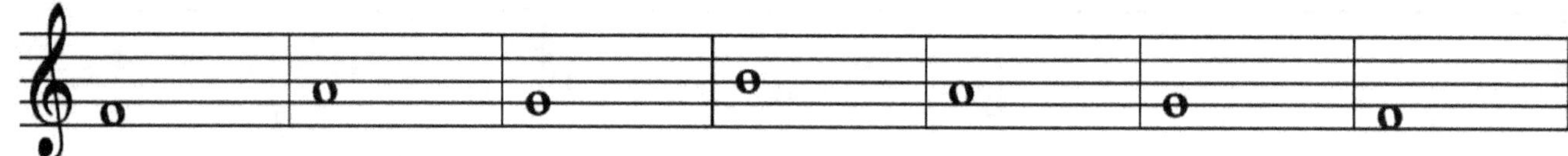

And now all seven notes

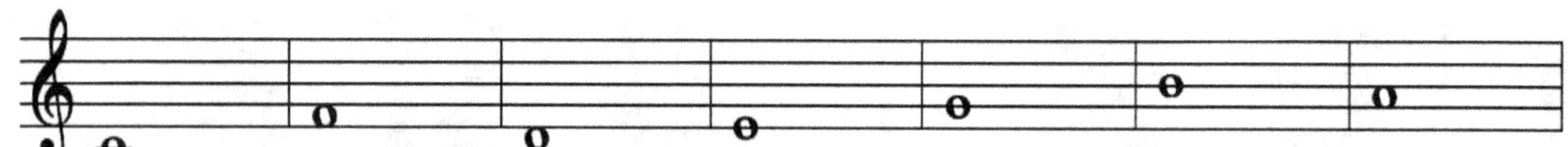

Note Values

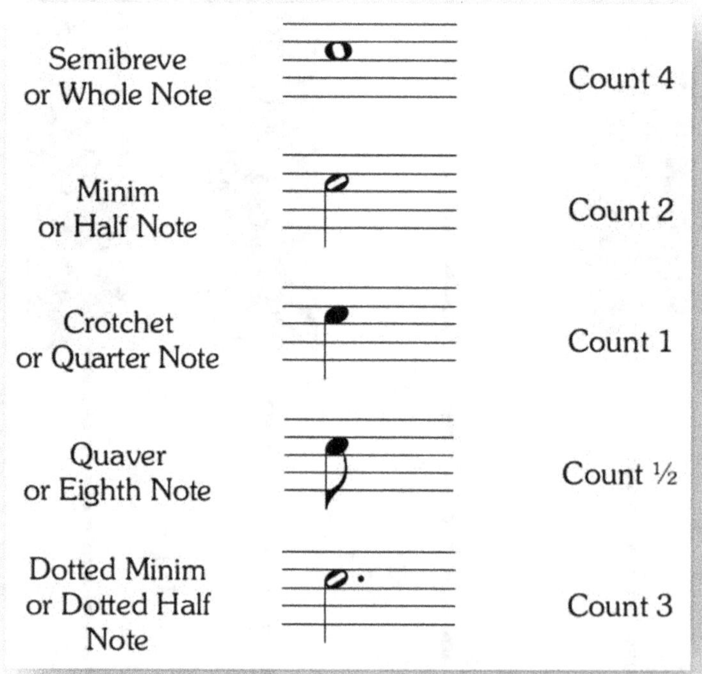

A dot after a note adds on half its value

Fingering

Hand and Fingering are as follows

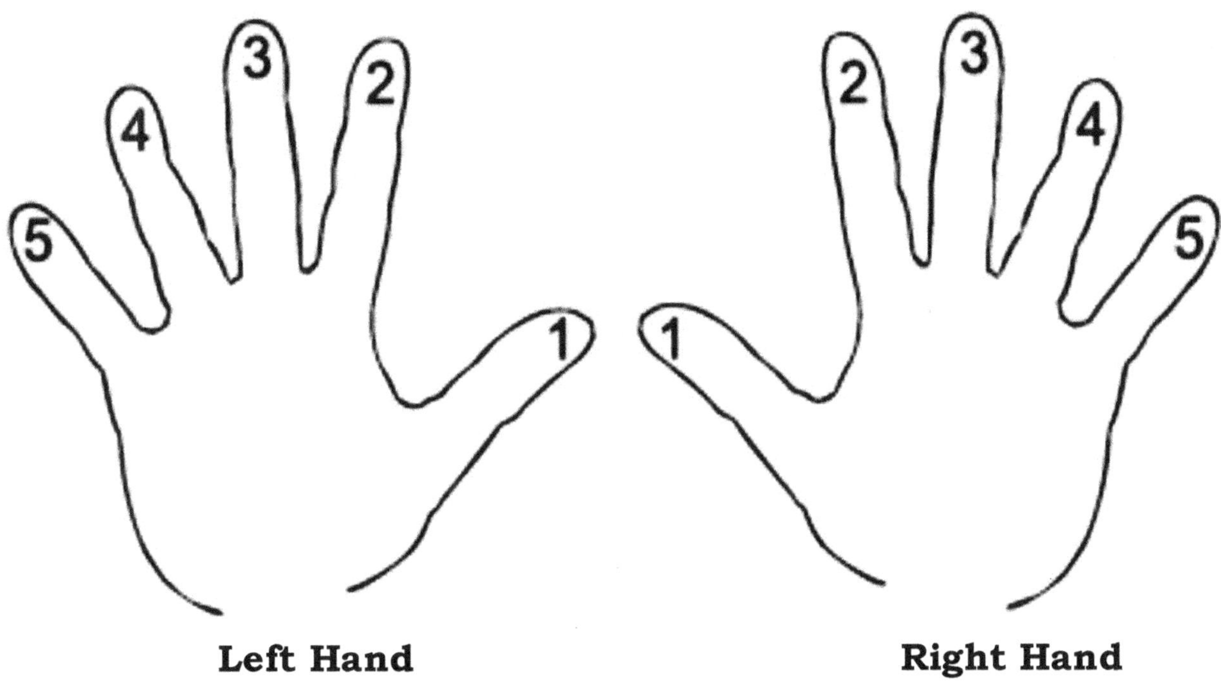

Pieces for the right hand, starting with the thumb

Chapter 2
Time Signatures and Rests

For the present the time signatures we will use are:

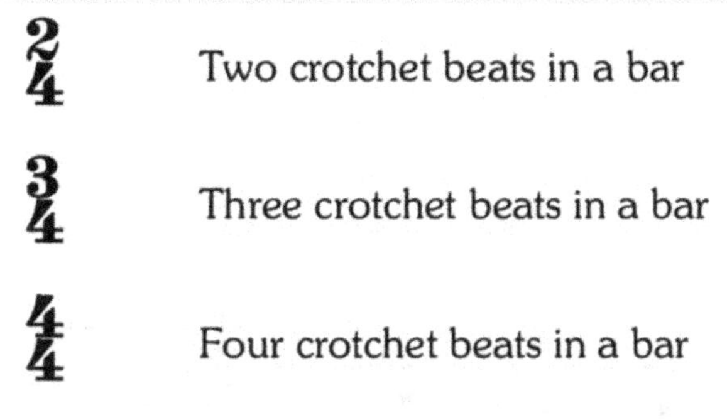

Silence, an important element in music, is indicated by *rests*, as follows:

Semibreve Rest		Silence for 4 beats
Minim Rest		Silence for 2 beats
Crotchet Rest		Silence for 1 beat
Quaver Rest		Silence for ½ beat
Dotted Minim Rest		Silence for 3 beats

A semibreve rest is used for a full bar's silence.

Pieces (right hand starting with the thumb)

Note that *barlines* divide the music into measures or bars, and that a double *barline* indicates the end of a piece.

Chapter 3
Treble and Bass Clefs

We need to extend our range of notes. You have seen the *treble clef* before. This sign is placed at the beginning of the *stave*, i.e. the lines and spaces on which the notes are written. In general the treble clef indicates notes for the right hand.

Treble Lines

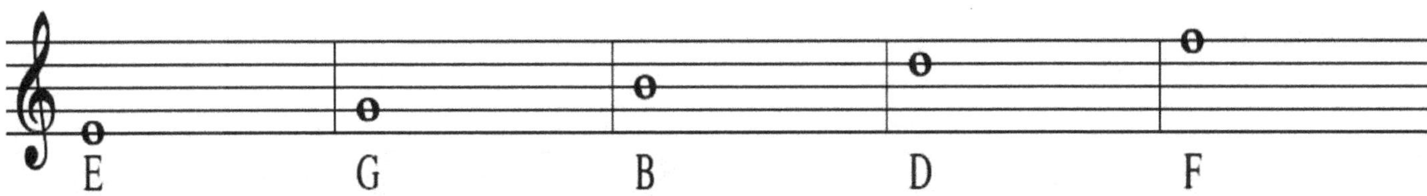

Treble Spaces

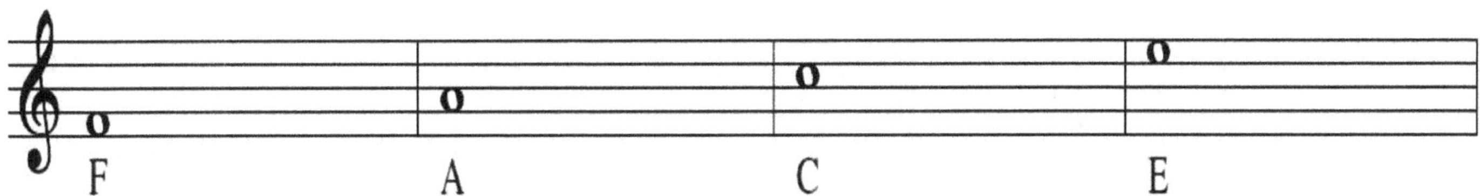

Middle C does not fit on the stave, so we place it on a *leger line* below the stave. The note D is placed just above this.

Bass clef and stave, used for left hand, and starting about one and a half octaves[1] below middle C, are:

Bass Lines

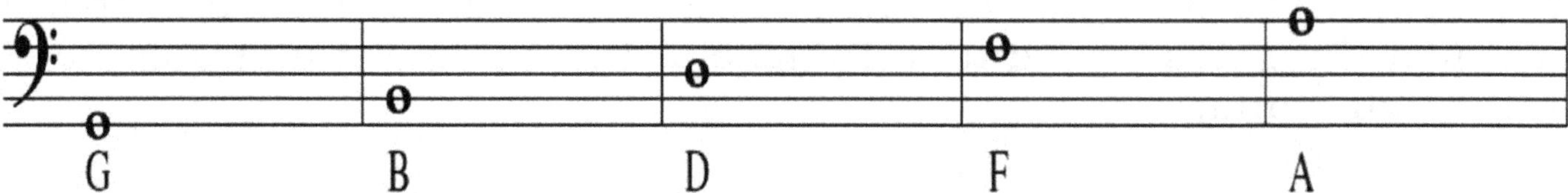

Bass spaces

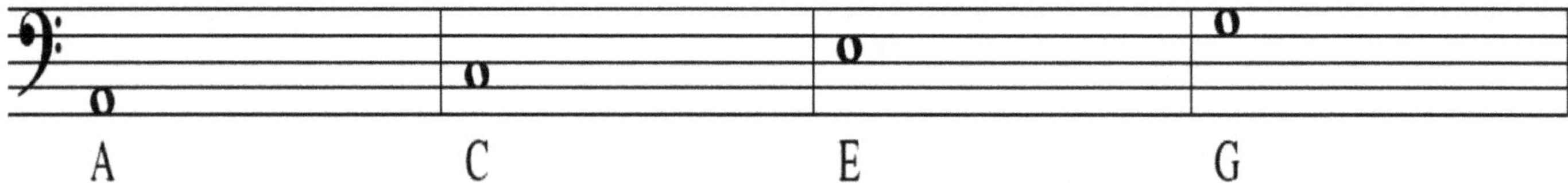

Middle C does not fit on the stave, so we place it on a leger line above the stave. The note B is placed just below this.

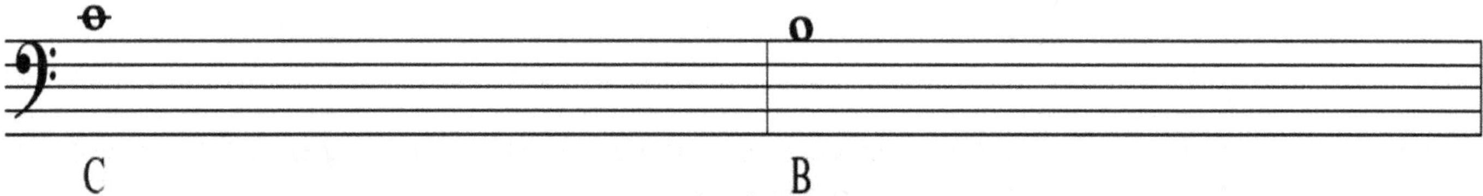

---

[1] C down to C forms an Octave

Note the introduction of fingering.

Here We Go

Walking Steadily

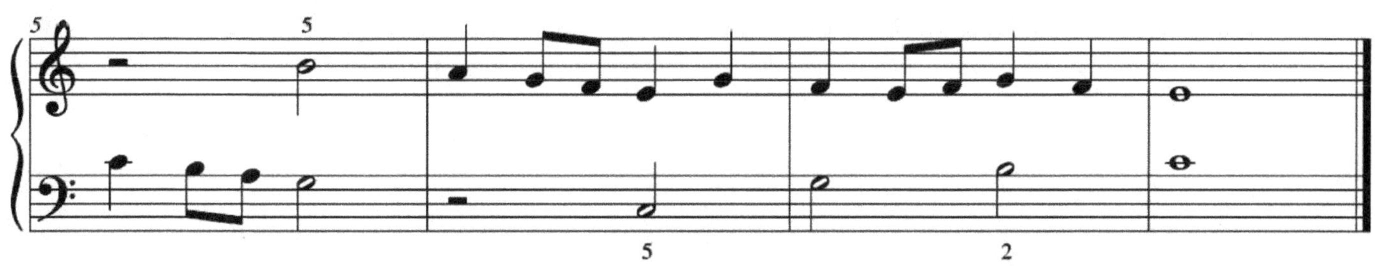

And Again

Chapter 4
Intervals, Scale and Chords
in Key of C Major

Before moving on we need a basic knowledge of intervals, i.e. the distance between one note and another.

Intervals in the bass are as follows:

Melodic

Harmonic

Intervals in the treble are as follows:

Melodic

Harmonic

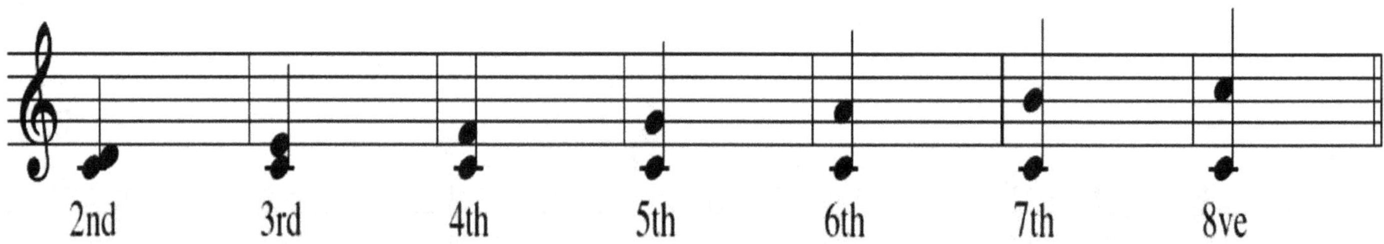

So far we have built our pieces from the key or scale of C Major.

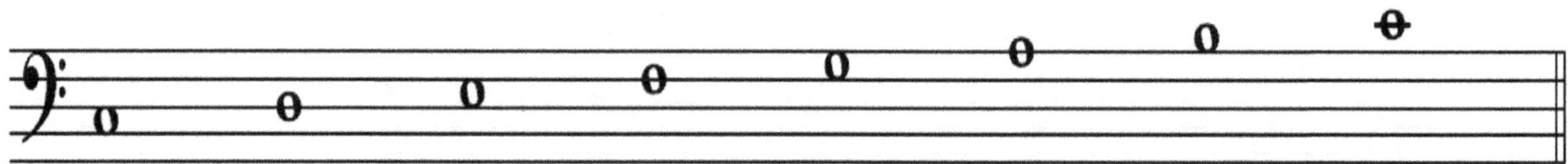

We will now introduce chords, which provide harmony to a melody in the key of C.

The principal chords are:

Chord I

Chord IV

Chord V

Other chords used are

Chord vi

and Chord ii

Harmony

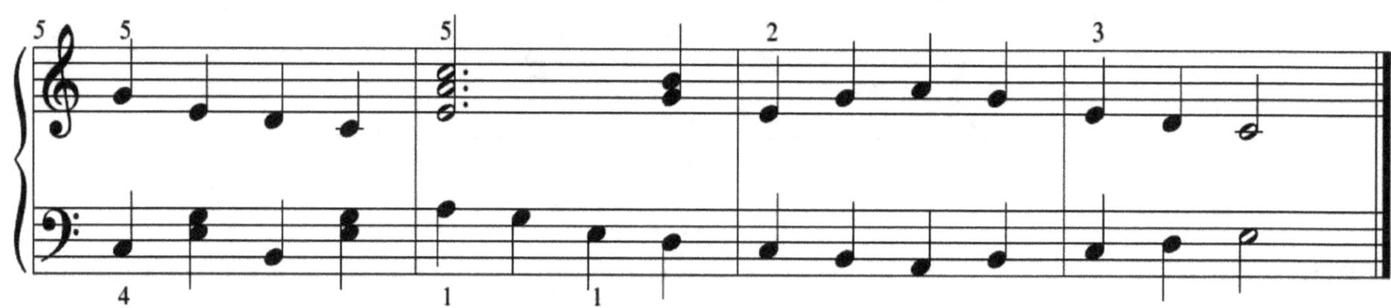

More Progress

Musing About Music Teaching

For a large proportion of my teaching experience, I taught music at St. Joseph's School for Visually Impaired, now ChildVision, Dublin. When I first took up the post, my thinking and practice were to give importance to the theoretical background and proceed from there. The response from my young Piano pupils was "I want to play a tune and chords". I quickly realised that I did not have the right to slow the process. Hence it came about that for many of those children playing was ahead of theory. Eventually, in some instances, quite interesting and original chord arrangements emerged from inventive students.

Depending on the particular student, the course pursued was towards examinations, i.e. Royal Irish Academy of Music grades and/or State Examinations Commission Junior and Leaving Certificate.

I have learned in my teaching that there is little difference in teaching blind or sighted children.

In general Braille music is taught to blind students and staff notation (possibly magnified) to children with low vision.

Braille music is not a simple matter. It has, however, logic and simplicity in conveying pitch. Instead of staff notation (which uses clefs and staves), octave signs are used, i.e. Octave 1 to Octave 7 starting with the note C as on piano or other keyboard instrument, and illustrated in Chapter 1 of this book.

This enables the teacher to deal with a mixed group of sighted and blind students, e.g. "4th octave C crotchet" indicates middle C crotchet.

When a brief explanation of clefs, treble and bass lines and spaces was given to one student in response to his query, his comment was "What a weird way of doing things".

Chapter 5
A New Key, Some More Signs, Expression Marks

The scale of G Major starts on the 5th note of the scale of C. To form this scale, we need to place a sharp sign before the note F as follows:

And with key signature

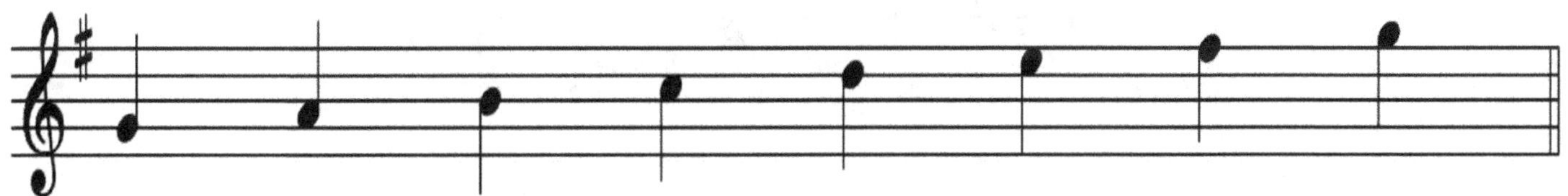

Principal chords

Chord I

Chord IV

Chord V

Other Chords

Chord vi

Chord ii

Before we proceed, it is necessary to explain some signs.

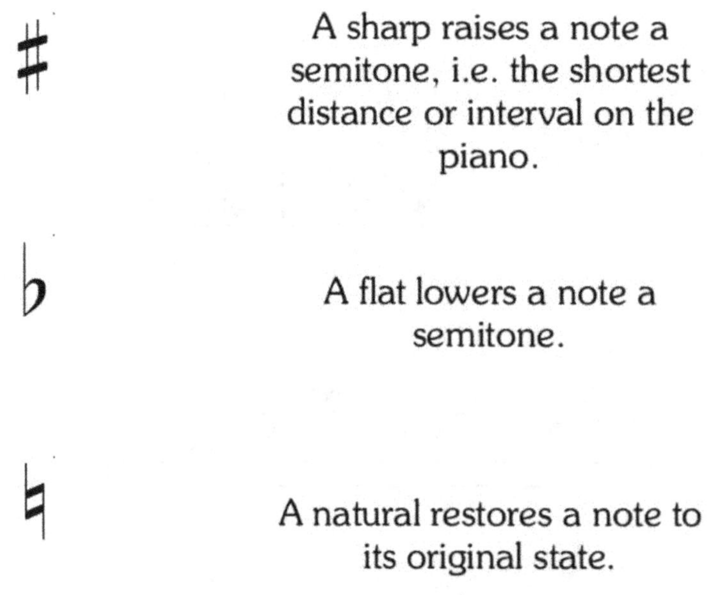

From here on, fingering is left to the performer or teacher. In some cases, there is more than one way of applying fingering.

Moving Up in Key

Some instructions on dynamics, tempo markings and articulation from the following tables are included in the next piece.

Dynamics

p	soft
mp	moderately soft
pp	very soft
f	loud
mf	moderately loud
ff	very loud
diminuendo [dim.]	becoming softer
crescendo [cresc.]	becoming louder

Tempo Markings

Allegretto	moderately fast
Allegro	fast
Andante	slow
Vivace	lively
ritenuto [rit.]	slower at once
a tempo	original pace

Articulation

Slur or legato — Join one note to the next

Staccato — Notes are detached

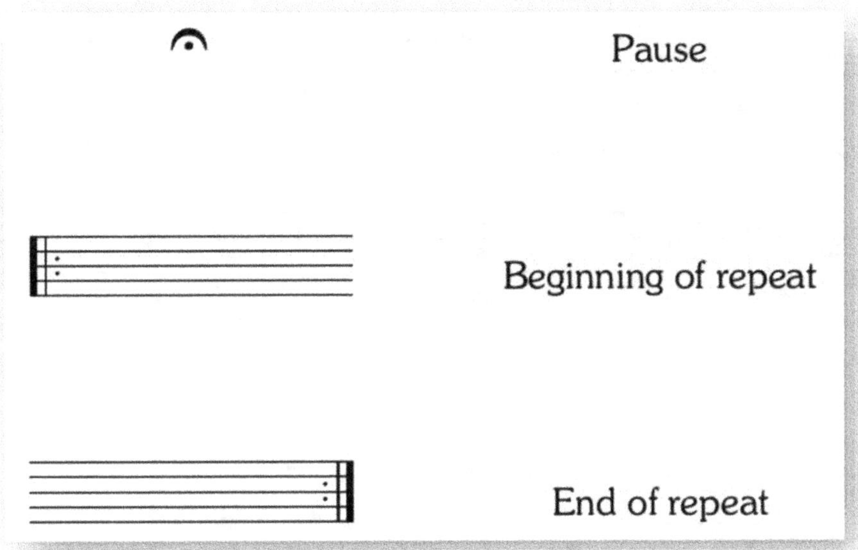

In bar 11 of the following piece, the note D in the right hand is joined by a tie to the same note in bar 12, i.e. the first D is played and held for the duration of both notes.

Lovely

Chapter 6
Key of D, More Leger Lines, Semiquaver, Triplet

Here, moving along the sharp side, we present the scale of D.

D Major starts on the 5th note of the scale of G, and has a new sharp, C sharp, on its 7th note.

Principal Chords

Chord I

Chord IV

Chord V

Other Chords

Chord vi

Chord ii

For our resources, we need more leger lines:

Treble Leger Lines

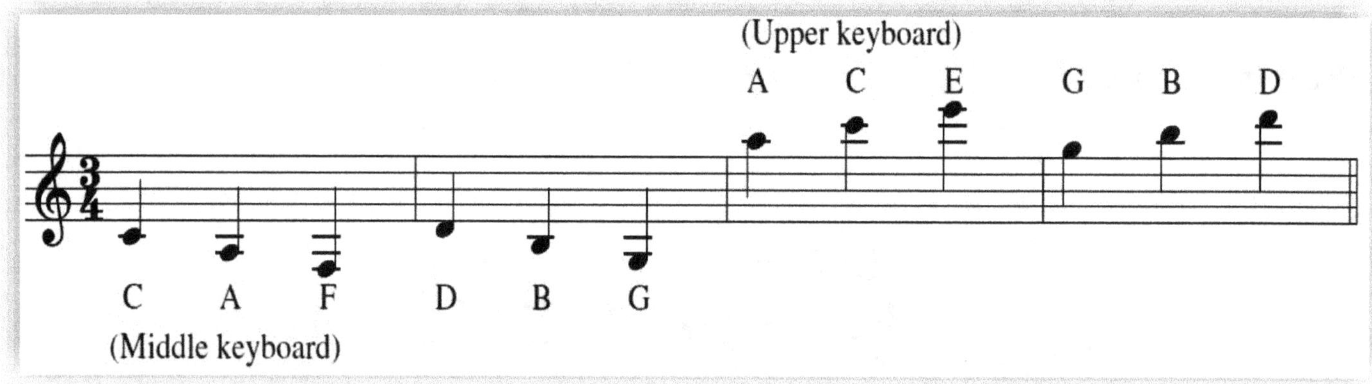

Bass Leger Lines

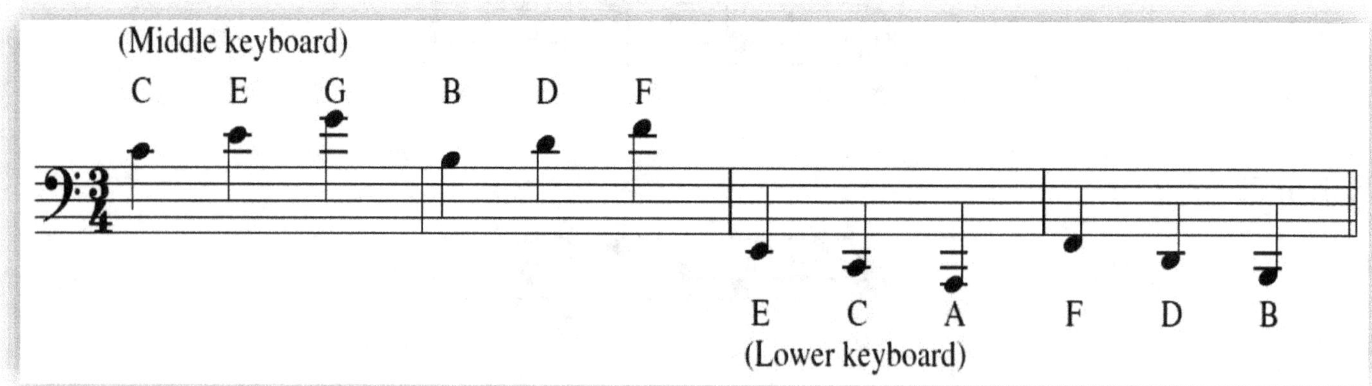

And more resources in duration:

♬	A semiquaver or sixteenth note lasts for ¼ beat.
𝄿	A semiquaver rest lasts for ¼ beat.
	A triplet indicates that three notes are to be played in the time of two such notes.

Combo

A Little Like Handel

Learning the Language

Another language which we call *Talk Music* has evolved, and is not to be dismissed. This language has been alluded to above where we spoke of "4th octave C crotchet" etc.

It is flexible, according to the ability and commitment of pupils, as well as to the growing experience of student and teacher.

We have encountered the language at workshops and seminars run by the Royal National Institute for the Blind in London, where talking scores are now produced.

We experimented with a written/brailled version, which we call *Type-Talk*, but as yet only to a small extent.

Insofar as we have used the language, it has been welcomed by lecturers in 3rd level Music Departments where our students have proceeded to study.

One student in particular enjoyed exploring this matter. When a doubt in the appropriate words to be used arose, he would say "We'll get down the big book", i.e. The New International Manual of Braille Music Notation. The language tends to mirror Braille as well as staff notation.

For now, and for the foreseeable future, Staff Notation is the music language used in vast areas of the world.

The aim of this book is to equip all music lovers and potential music lovers with this language.

Chapter 7
Key of F, Six-eight time, Phrasing

The scale of F major starts on the 4th note of the scale of C.

F major has one flat, B flat, its 4th note.

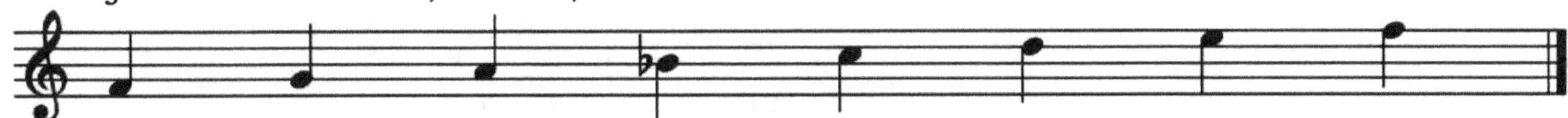

With key signature

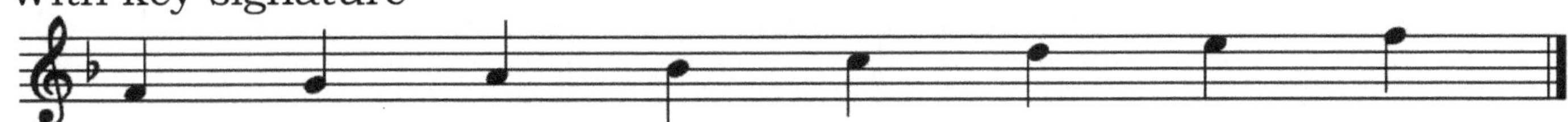

Principal Chords

Chord I

Chord IV

Chord V

Other Chords

Chord vi

Chord ii

A New Time Signature

$\dfrac{6}{8}$

This time signature indicates that there are two dotted crotchet beats in a bar.
This is equal to six quavers.

Moving to the Flat Side

The long, curved lines above are phrase marks. Phrase marks end with
cadences. Cadences to which we give attention here are perfect cadence,
chord V-I (bars 15-16), and imperfect cadence, chord vi-V (bars 7-8). A
perfect cadence indicates a final ending, an imperfect cadence indicates a
less final ending.

Not So Even

Chapter 8
The Minor Scale

Every major scale has a relative minor. The minor scale starts on the 6th note of the major scale. A minor is the relative of C major. We need to raise the 7th note of the minor scale by a chromatic semitone, i.e. G to G sharp. This is the harmonic minor scale.

Principal Chords

Chord i

Chord iv

Chord V

Another Chord

Chord VI

Use of chord ii in the minor is restricted.

Proceeding on the sharp side, E minor is the relative of G major.

Principal Chords

Chord i

Chord iv

Chord V

Another Chord

Chord VI

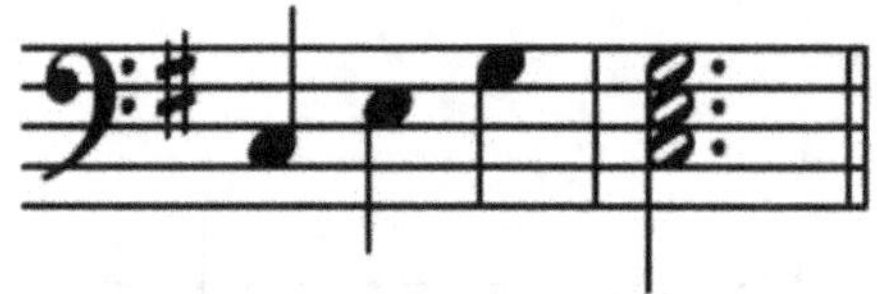

And on the flat side, D minor is the relative of F major.

Principal Chords

Chord i

Chord iv

Chord V

Another Chord

Chord VI

Sombre Stroll

A Song For Devin

In bar 7 of A Song for Devin (in E minor) you have use of the melodic minor scale ascending. In bar 5 you have use of the same scale descending. The purpose is to provide for an easier flow of melody. Note the difference between this and the scale of E harmonic minor (p. 38).

A Little Adventurous

In bars 5-6 of A Little Adventurous (in D minor) there is a modulation or change of key to B flat major; this is a related key. There follows a modulation to A flat major; this is not a related key, but the piece seems to want to go there. Related keys are explained in Appendix I.

Chapter 9
B Flat Major, G Minor,
B Minor, The Modal Scale

B flat major has 2 flats, B flat and E flat.

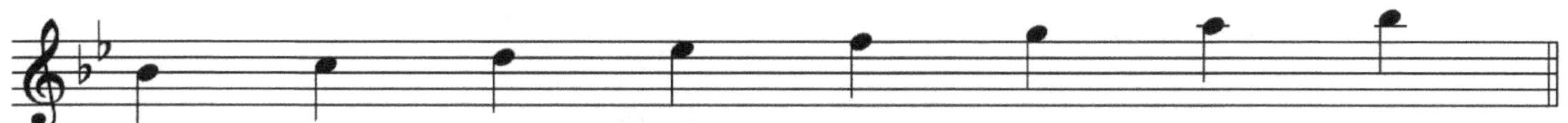

Principal Chords

Chord I

Chord IV

Chord V

Other Chords

Chord vi

Chord ii

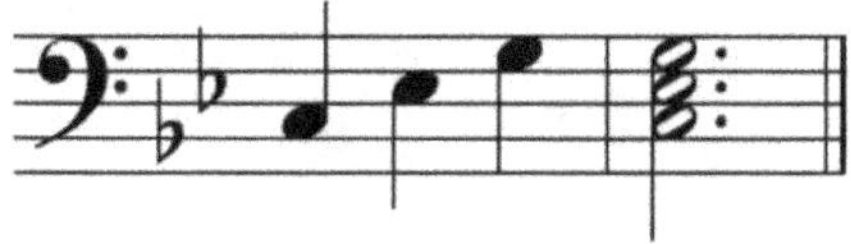

The relative minor is G minor.

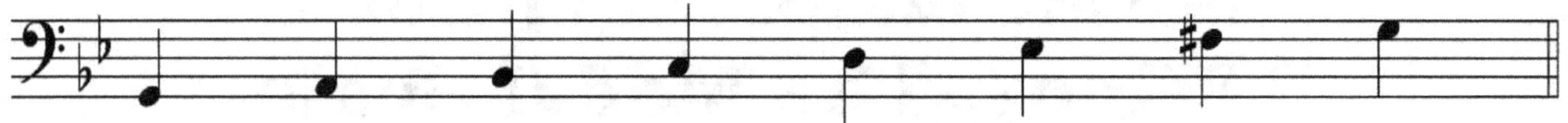

Principal Chords

Chord i

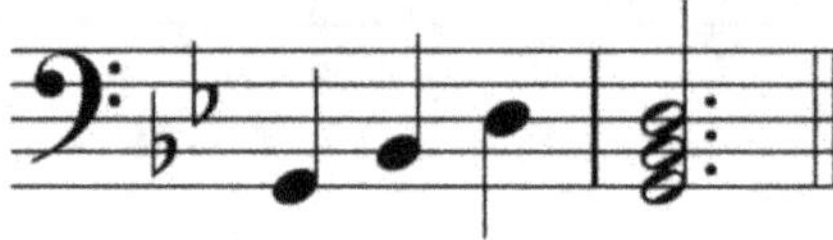

Chord iv

Chord V

Another Chord

Chord VI

To even up matters on the sharp side, B minor is the relative of D major.

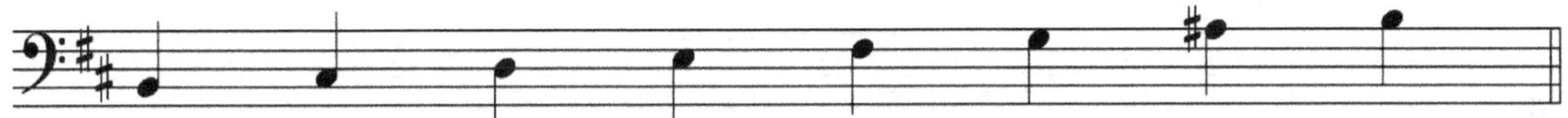

Principal Chords

Chord i

Chord iv

Chord V

Another Chord

Chord VI

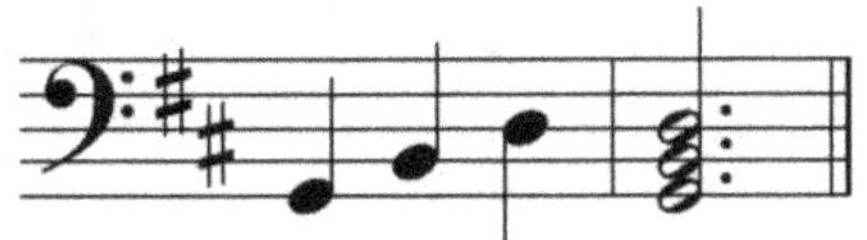

More Adventure

Peacefully

For theoretical reasons, and because we may come across these scales or keys, remaining scales, major and minor up to 4 sharps and 4 flats are set out in Appendix II.

And before we finish, some modal scales; these can be explained through the white notes of the keyboard.

Modal Scales

Furthermore, modal scales can be transposed:

Dorian mode transposed up a fifth

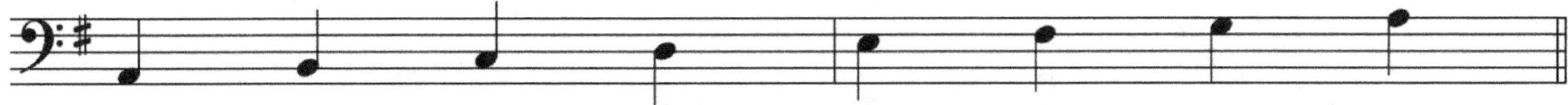

Aeolian mode transposed up a fourth

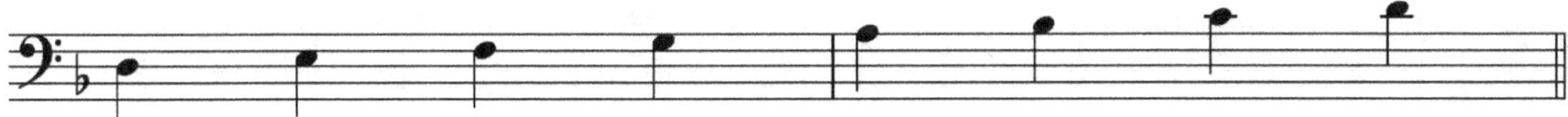

If you check the position of the semitones, you will discover that they occur in the same position as in the original scales.

Thinking of Scales

Did you think that scales are monotonous? Knowledge and understanding of scales provide us with an endless source in the study and making of music.

Jaunting Along

Quietly

Chapter 10
Conclusion

To complete our brief, this chapter presents three Irish ballads, as well as a song of tribute to a sweet young girl.

The ballads were learned by me as a child from my father, who was steeped in Irish history, at the same time aware of its complexity.

Marioara came to our country for opportunity, only to have her dreams trampled underfoot. "Sweet dreams Little One".

Finally, there is Ellis Island, inspired by a visit there in October 2011. This song is a salute to those who left our land over the years in search of a better life. Many prospered; some did not. To all of these, our people, Beannachtai na bhflaitheas oraibh.

Foggy Dew

Carrickfergus

Eamon an Chnuic

Little One

Ellis Island

Appendix I

Related Keys

Each degree of the scale has a name, which is common to all scales, as follows:

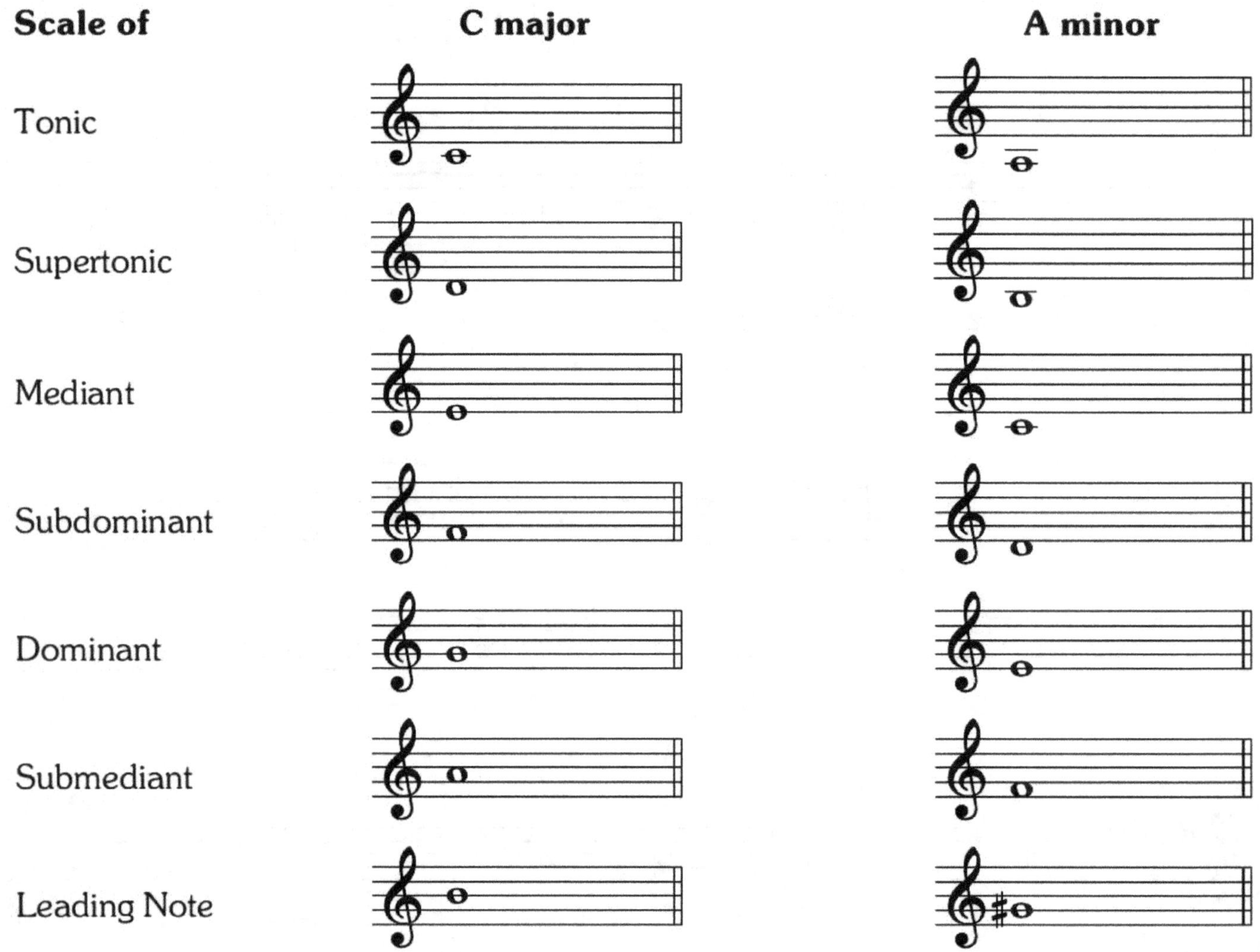

Keys related to the major key or scale are its relative minor, its subdominant, dominant and the relative minors of each of these two. Hence keys related to C major are A minor, F major, G major, D minor and E minor.

Keys related to the minor scale are its relative major, its subdominant and dominant and the relative majors of each of these two. Hence the relatives of A minor are C major, D minor, E minor, F major and G major.

Appendix II

More scales

A Major

F Sharp Minor

E Major

C Sharp Minor

E Flat Major

C Minor

A Flat Major

F Minor